Dear Parent:
Your child's love of reading s...

Every child learns to read in a different way and at his or her own speed. Some go back and forth between reading levels and read favourite books again and again. Others read through each level in order. You can help your young reader improve and become more confident by encouraging his or her own interests and abilities. From books your child reads with you to the first books he or she reads alone, there are I Can Read Books for every stage of reading:

SHARED READING
Basic language, word repetition, and whimsical illustrations, ideal for sharing with your emergent reader

BEGINNING READING
Short sentences, familiar words, and simple concepts for children eager to read on their own

READING WITH HELP
Engaging stories, longer sentences, and language play for developing readers

READING ALONE
Complex plots, challenging vocabulary, and high-interest topics for the independent reader

ADVANCED READING
Short paragraphs, chapters, and exciting themes for the perfect bridge to chapter books

I Can Read Books have introduced children to the joy of reading since 1957. Featuring award-winning authors and illustrators and a fabulous cast of beloved characters, I Can Read Books set the standard for beginning readers.

A lifetime of discovery begins with the magical words **"I Can Read!"**

Visit www.icanread.ca for information
on enriching your child's reading experience.

I Can Read Book® is a trademark of HarperCollins Publishers

What's in a Number?
Text copyright © 2019 by HarperCollins Publishers Ltd.
Illustrations © 2019 by Nick Craine.
All rights reserved. Published by Collins, an imprint of HarperCollins Publishers Ltd

HarperCollins books may be purchased for educational, business, or sales promotional use through our Special Markets Department.

HarperCollins Publishers Ltd
Bay Adelaide Centre, East Tower
22 Adelaide Street West, 41st Floor
Toronto, Ontario, Canada
M5H 4E3

www.harpercollins.ca

Library and Archives Canada Cataloguing in Publication information is available upon request.

www.icanread.ca

ISBN 978-1-4434-5731-6

WZL 1 2 3 4 5 6 7 8 9 10

WHAT'S IN

A NUMBER?

by Meg Braithwaite

Illustrations by Nick Craine

Collins

Only a few NHL players have worn the number 99.

Do you know who

the most famous one was?

Yes, it's Wayne Gretzky!

That number was special to Wayne.

Wayne's favourite hockey player
was Gordie Howe.
And Gordie wore number 9.

Wayne asked for number 9

whenever he could.

And he usually got it.

But then Wayne started

junior hockey.

The number 9 was already taken.

Oh no!

Wayne was sad.

So his coach said,

"Why not wear two 9s?"

"Good idea!" Wayne said.

He had 99 stitched on his sweater.

Lots of NHL players pick
numbers for special reasons.
Sometimes it's for the same
reason as Wayne.

They pick the numbers

their heroes wore.

Jonathan's favourite player wore the number 19.

So Jonathan wears 19 too.

Sometimes players pick numbers that people in their family wore.

Auston's grandpa
played basketball in college.
So Auston wears 34,
just like his grandpa did.

Alex's grandma

played basketball at the Olympics.

So Alex wears 8 like she did.

But players choose numbers
for other reasons too.

Sidney picked the number 87
because he was born in 1987.

Jordin Tootoo's last name sounds
like "two-two."
So he wears the number 22.

But players can't always get
the numbers they want.

John couldn't use the number 19.

So he flipped it around to 91.

Russ couldn't get the number 9.

So he turned it upside down.

He wore a 6.

Mario did the same thing.

He wore 66 to honour Wayne Gretzky.

Pierre wanted the number 10.

But the number 10 was being used.

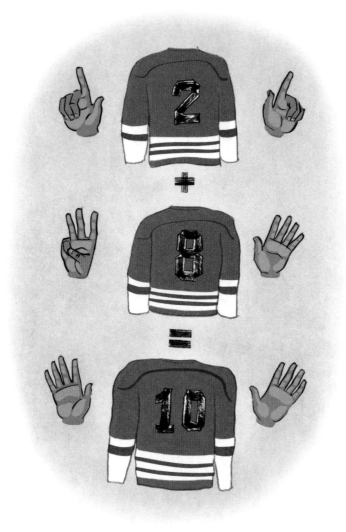

So Pierre chose 28.

Why?

Because 2 plus 8 equals 10.

Maurice chose a number
for his daughter.

She weighed nine pounds when
she was born.
So he chose the number 9.

But there's one number that
no hockey player will ever
wear again.

That's Wayne's number 99.

The NHL decided Wayne would

be the last one to wear it.

He was that good.

What number would you choose if you were in the NHL?